Selling You[r]

How 8 Business Owners Transformed Their Lives

TABLE OF CONTENTS

	Welcome to Woodbridge International	1
Chapter 1	**The Sommelier Company** EVENTS	5
Chapter 2	**Tuscan Imports** HOUSEHOLD APPLIANCES	13
Chapter 3	**Prime Techology** ELECTRONIC COMPONENT MANUFACTURING	21
Chapter 4	**Paragon Corvette Reproductions** AUTOMOTIVE PARTS MANUFACTURING	29
Chapter 5	**Northeast Work & Safety Boats** RIVER & MARINE SERVICES	37
Chapter 6	**Knowledge Matters** IT SERVICES	45
Chapter 7	**Amuze Products** VENDING SERVICES	53
Chapter 8	**Alternative Exports** INTERNATIONAL DISTRIBUTOR	61

Welcome to Woodbridge International

Robert Koenig
Founder and CEO

Woodbridge
International
Mergers & Acquisitions Since 1993

Woodbridge International
Robert Koenig

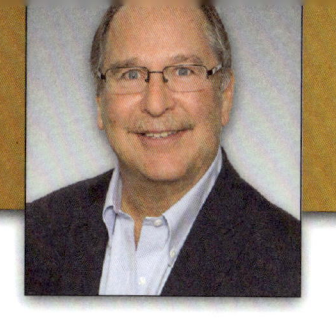

I started Woodbridge International in April 1993, almost 30 years ago. Since then, we have become the gold standard for global mid-market mergers and acquisitions. There is no other firm serving companies with under $250 million in revenue that can outperform our auction process, global reach, and technology – not to mention our proprietary email database, management meeting training, and talented team.

While we're proud of our successes and celebrate them, like you, we never rest on our achievements, and are continually pushing the boundaries of our industry just as we did back in 1993. One thing hasn't changed – our mission. We continue to positively transform the lives of business owners.

Our Purpose Is to Transform Your Life

Selling your business is a life-changing event, one that doesn't come without its share of hard-earned rewards. While most business owners feel a surge of relief and freedom after a sale, others are left with a sense that now that they've sold, they don't want to disengage entirely.

Each of the eight business owners profiled in this book took a different path after the sale. They come from a wide range of industries, backgrounds, and experiences. Some never said goodbye and continue to run the business under new ownership with added resources. Others successfully took on a new role to focus again on their true passion, while several walked away content in the knowledge that they took care of their employees and their business before starting the next chapter of their lives. Each of these stories reminds us that our process is powerful, it works, and it can help you move forward with your next life adventure.

As you'll see in each of these stories, saying goodbye to your business and your team can be complicated, filled with emotional highs and lows. This can be avoided with early, purpose-driven planning. You can do good by those who have served you so well – your employees, customers, suppliers, and the larger industry – with positive impacts across the deal spectrum: retaining an enthusiastic workforce, customers willing to stay on (which will naturally reflect on the business' valuation), and other benefits such as real estate opportunities, stronger partnerships, and the multiplier effect of positive PR and marketing.

A company isn't just an instrument that generates money – an asset to liquidate when it comes time to cash out – but a unique ecosystem that shapes the lives of many. It's an integral part of both your identity as well as the center of your team's very purpose. And, more often than not, your business is a family, a tight-knit crew deeply devoted to your company's mission and its enduring success.

They are the people who supply the energy, the creativity, and the passion which allow your firm to thrive. Developing a legacy-driven mindset will help both to define the cultural dynamic and sustain your team through the challenges as well as the opportunities that lie ahead.

When you decide it is time to sell, it's never too early to create a framework that fits your organization's culture and ensures your team is taken care of throughout the transition and into the future, as a master builder of change. Organizational health should be a top priority alongside economic and financial objectives. The emotional well-being of your team, including environment, mission, value, ethics, expectations, and goals, if managed from the outset, can ground your firm and provide a huge advantage to a buyer as you confidently pass the torch. As a seller, you must navigate myriad questions and changes that will come and eventually create a path of your own.

The landscape is always evolving in unexpected ways. No one can predict the future, or how interest can shift from one segment to another. No matter what kind of deal you ultimately strike with a buyer, when it's time to sell, gratitude, generosity, and graciousness never go out of style, and will be appreciated long after your business changes hands.

The Woodbridge International team wishes you much success.

WOODBRIDGE
International
Mergers & Acquisitions Since 1993

Chapter 1

> "I could use a personal change – I'm a business school professor at Chapman University and I own some other companies, and life is short. It's very easy for me to just continue working around the clock."

Jörn "Joey" Kleinhans
The Sommelier Company

WOODBRIDGE *International*
Mergers & Acquisitions Since 1993

The Sommelier Company
EVENTS

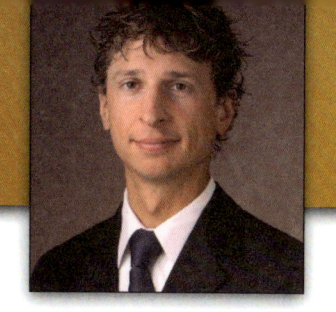

To Jörn "Joey" Kleinhans, having the freedom to follow a passion is what makes life worth living. "I've always felt that a free man should work for himself," says the founder of The Sommelier Company, the premier provider of wine and spirits expertise and guided tasting events.

It was during his tenure as Vice President at PIMCO, at that time the world's biggest bond trading house, that Kleinhans began to feel his career in the investment industry had run its course (by that time, Kleinhans had held management roles at INVESCO and KPMG, too). The entrepreneur shares his thoughts on motivation and ideas:

> "If someone else has a goal, I can certainly do the necessary work, but I can only do a fraction of the quality of the work that I can do if it's my own idea. I think some people are wired like that. If it's your idea, you're going to be much more behind it…I found out about that mechanism between me having an idea, and then me running with that idea, being very powerful in terms of how I care about it, and how good the results are."

Bringing the experts and their audience together

It was in this frame of mind that Kleinhans went ahead with starting The Sommelier Company. He had long been interested in wine, and in having experts share their knowledge with him. What if those experts could be hired for private events and interact with audiences that shared their passion? Kleinhans suspected that there was an enormous appetite for wine knowledge in the U.S., but that the country didn't have a well-developed culture of engaging with its sommeliers. He'd identified the gap in the market and set about filling it.

The first step was to build a website. Kleinhans used SEO techniques to ensure that The Sommelier Company was the top result for all relevant searches. From that point on, the number of inbound leads generated by the company's website grew steadily so that Kleinhans stopped traveling around the U.S. trying to sell the services in person. The entrepreneur acknowledges that this approach is "somewhat unintuitive," but the proof is in the pudding: Focusing "on those people in society who are already interested" definitely worked for The Sommelier Company.

Don't undervalue your product

Once he'd established an online presence for his company, Kleinhans began to interact with interested prospects daily. However, he wasn't interested in those who weren't willing to pay what he believed to be the right price. On how he managed to overcome the pricing hurdle, Kleinhans has the following insight:

> "Confidence. The bigger the number, the better the product. It is often a mistake to believe that people can't pay for something. It usually means that you haven't made clear how good, great, or useful the product is. So, whenever someone told me 'This is completely overpriced,' I increased the price and got rid of those who can't pay for it. Turns out that the equilibrium price for this product is much higher than I initially expected."

The Sommelier Company grew slowly for the first few years, but when the pandemic hit, business boomed. Because the company had been doing virtual wine tasting events pre-pandemic, it was able to rapidly scale up to a fully remote service offering. Despite in-person events being permitted in most of the U.S. as of 2021, the company has continued to offer virtual events in addition to in-person events, as they can often be more cost efficient for corporate clients.

Of its pandemic growth and what that meant for him as the owner, Kleinhans says:

> *"My plan was never to sell the company, but last fall things grew so fast. And that was also tough on me. Working around the clock. And how is that going to continue? What if the company continues to grow? Am I just going to work myself into an early grave? If I own the company 100%, it has to go my way. Even if I have a larger team, I have to understand if everything is going well, because I am responsible. And it's all my money, too. And so, unloading part of the responsibility was part of the appeal."*

The growth The Sommelier Company experienced in 2020 recategorized it as a middle-market business, and Kleinhans began thinking about selling. "A company founder is often very good at starting something and bringing it from zero to one but may not necessarily be the best person for bringing it from one to infinity," says the wine enthusiast.

Cast a wide net to catch the right buyer

The entrepreneur interviewed four M&A firms specializing in middle-market deals. His decision to work with Woodbridge International was driven by the firm's mass-market approach to finding a buyer. Where traditional M&A firms typically rely on a list of fewer than 100 contacts, Woodbridge has built up a database of approximately 15,000 financial and strategic buyers. "I know how hard it is to sell something – you've got to talk to 100 people before you even find a couple of people who are halfway interested," says Kleinhans of the marketing process.

Another unique aspect of the Woodbridge offering is its two-day management meeting training program, geared toward helping business owners understand what the expectations of potential buyers will be. Off the back of the training, which Kleinhans found to be "very insightful," he received letters of intent from the majority of the parties he attended management meetings with.

Handing over a well-functioning business is part of the deal

The Sommelier Company was acquired by Vintage Wine Estates, a Nasdaq-listed U.S. wine producer, in June 2021. Kleinhans is staying on in a consulting capacity for an agreed-upon transition period and is training the people who will take over from him eventually. "It's simply part of the promise when you sell a company – there is the implicit promise that you hand it over properly and set up the new owners for long-term success," says Kleinhans. For the entrepreneur, life hasn't changed yet, but he's sure the change is coming. Kleinhans looks forward to the personal change that his changing role at The Sommelier Company will represent.

Having gone through the sale process, Kleinhans cautions other business owners not to presume that they'll be able to walk away from their companies the minute the deal goes through:

> *"I would definitely not give owners the hope that they can just walk away from the company when they sell it. It may happen in rare circumstances, but in most cases the new owners will need the further assistance of the founder. The founder is often a driver of the business, and the new owners will want to make sure they can extract that information over a transition period."*

Woodbridge promised, and delivered, a short, disciplined timeline. Kleinhans can hardly believe that it's only been nine months since he first considered selling The Sommelier Company. "It's really a miracle," he says.

June 2021

The Sommelier Company
Huntington Beach, California

was acquired by

VWE
VINTAGE WINE ESTATES

Vintage Wine Estates, Inc.
Santa Rosa, California

The undersigned acted as advisor to The Sommelier Company

WOODBRIDGE
International

1764 Litchfield Turnpike | Suite 250 | New Haven, CT 06525
203.389.8400 | woodbridgegrp.com

Chapter 2

" We are very passionate about the product, and I think that has really been the major aspect that has helped us grow the business. We just loved what we were building. "

Kirk Laing
Tuscan Imports

If you had to pick three words to define Italian culture, there's a good chance you'd go with "family, food, and community." While living in Italy, ordained minister and bible studies graduate Kirk Laing and his family – half of whom are Italian – grew to love the togetherness represented by Italian culture. In 1998, after eight years of living just outside Florence, however, a move back to the U.S. became necessary. Two weeks later, Kirk was thrust into the role of entrepreneur after an accident resulted in his daughter becoming dependent on a ventilator.

"Everything was new as far as my daughter and her medical situation. We had no idea what that would entail. I was basically operating the business out of my backyard so I could be close to home," says Kirk. Despite not having a background in business management, Kirk founded Tuscan Imports, which went on to become a leading distributor of Italian ovens, grills, and decorative terracotta pottery.

The idea behind the business was rooted in the family's experience of living in Italy: Food and cooking bringing friends and family together. As the company grew, Kirk started selling out of his truck, traveling across the Southeast and spending his days on the road. "It was a matter of survival. I just had to make ends meet," he says.

Building a globally recognized brand

Kirk's approach to relationships was a key factor in his success. "We have really built our business on integrity and honesty. If we can't do it correctly, there's no reason to do it at all. For Tuscan Imports, the company is about more than pushing numbers, it's about connecting with customers. We are very passionate about the product that we have. And I think that has really been the major aspect that has helped us grow," says Kirk.

Kirk's son Philip reflects on how far Tuscan Imports has come since his childhood: "My father's been able to build this business, not just as an entrepreneur and a business-minded manager, but starting with the basic ordering, the labor, the delivery – he's done everything from the very beginning."

Since its inception in 1998, the 100% family-run company's exceptional product knowledge and focus on exemplary customer satisfaction has earned them an excellent reputation. As a testament to this, Tuscan Imports has grown through two recessions.

Knowing when the business is sellable

Until 2020, Kirk and his family didn't think Tuscan Imports could be sold. "The business grew to the point where we were overwhelmed. We felt like we were doing everything we could just to keep our heads above water. A lot of businesses were hurting during COVID-19 – our business jumped by 40%. We knew that to take it to the next level, we probably needed somebody more experienced than us," says Kirk. The entrepreneur's family also knew that Kirk needed a break. "He's been working since 1998, watching the steady growth, but it was a continuous stretch; just constantly working and increasing the workload," says Philip.

Tuscan Imports had never gone to market before. "Woodbridge told us our company was marketable and that they could find a buyer, so we opted to pursue that avenue. Right now, I'm still in a state of disbelief and a little bit numb," he said.

Kirk called Larry Reinharz at Woodbridge to test the waters. He described the company to the M&A firm and gave a synopsis of their financials. "Larry's response was that the business was absolutely sellable. And at that point we really started moving forward. I was skeptical throughout the whole process. I had my doubts the entire time," said Kirk. He called previous clients who had sold their companies through Woodbridge International for referrals. "I did not talk to any other M&A firms. The referrals were good, I felt confident with what Larry told me, and I felt comfortable with what I saw online, and we decided to move forward," said Kirk. He knew Tuscan Imports was making money and growing. He signed with Woodbridge International in August 2020 and went to market in October that same year.

Finding the perfect suitor

Tuscan Imports' objective was to find a buyer who could assist with the employees who were staying on, along with its representatives and manufacturers. The transition had to be seamless. "My main goal was making sure that everybody who was working with us – whether it was employees or vendors – that things would continue to run smoothly for them, and that they would be taken care of," says Kirk.

As the campaign took shape, Kirk realized that he was about to sell his "baby." "My wife asked me, is this going to be difficult for you? This has been your baby for many years, and my response has always been, no, not at all. Because I don't find my identity in the business. We enjoy what we're doing. As far as letting go, even now in the transition, it's not difficult for me," says Kirk.

As management meetings kicked off, Kirk and Philip realized they were selling the company and needed to pitch Tuscan Imports. "It's hard for us to pat ourselves on the back and talk about how good of a job we've done. But we also recognized that we were actually selling the business. So, we had to portray the business as something very marketable, a business that is growing, and that there's a lot of opportunity. Woodbridge really helped us in seeing it that way, because our tendency is to downplay it more than to put a real positive spin on it," says Kirk.

Understanding and communicating the value of your business

In April 2021, Tuscan Imports was acquired by Salt Creek Capital. "The process was very quick. It was more work than I thought it was going to be, because we were running a business at the same time. But I would say other than that it did go very smoothly," says Kirk.

Philip's advice to entrepreneurs who are considering selling their company is, "Don't sell yourself short. For some people it's just about numbers, this is what it's worth period, versus being able to attempt to transfer that passion. Hopefully a business owner is passionate about what they've built – this is something they've created – and can express the passion, the desire, and the belief in the business and sell that along with the numbers," said Philip.

By recording a video viewed by potential buyers, Tuscan Imports was able to share their love for the business in the sales process. "I think that may have helped us, even being a business that isn't a huge conglomerate where the numbers just speak for themselves. But I think even with a bigger business, having somebody that can do that eloquently and properly and efficiently, would be very helpful," says Philip.

Getting to a position where you can help people

Now that Tuscan Imports has been sold, Kirk looks forward to doing things he never had the time or opportunity to do. "I don't think this is going to change us one bit. I think we're still the same people, we're going to remain the same people, we're not going to live any differently. We're thankful. But we also feel like with the sale of the business, and with the success of the business, we're responsible. We've been given much and so we're responsible to give back."

April 2021

TUSCAN IMPORTS
HAND-CRAFTED ITALIAN TERRACOTTA & STONE PRODUCTS

Tuscan Imports, Inc.
Florence, South Carolina

has been acquired by

Salt Creek Capital

Salt Creek Capital
Woodside, California

The undersigned acted as advisor to Tuscan Imports, Inc.

WOODBRIDGE
International

1764 Litchfield Turnpike | Suite 250 | New Haven, CT 06525
203.389.8400 | woodbridgegrp.com

Chapter 3

"When we realized that there was not a good succession plan, that's when we confronted the idea of selling the company. Because we created it, we don't want to see it disappear."

Luis Lluberes
Prime Technology

WOODBRIDGE
International
Mergers & Acquisitions Since 1993

Prime Technology
ELECTRONIC COMPONENT MANUFACTURING

Since its inception in 1973, more than 40 years ago, Prime Technology has grown to become a key supplier of instrumentation to the U.S. and Royal Navies, as well as a host of large commercial clients. The company began life in Mt. Vernon, New York, relocated to North Branford, Connecticut in 1982, and opened a facility in the Dominican Republic in 1986. The Connecticut facility is now 36,000 square feet in size, and the Dominican facility measures over 20,000 square feet.

Outgoing President and COO Luis Lluberes joined in 1986, soon after the company had opened its Dominican Republic facility. Lluberes recalls a decisive moment in the company's history: "In 1999, we were awarded a contract to supply all the instrumentation for the U.S. Navy's Virginia-class submarines. Prime Technology immediately experienced a quantum leap in growth." The Navy contract was a big commitment for the company and led to Lluberes and several other employees becoming shareholders.

Commitment increases when employees become shareholders

"Being an owner gives you another level of understanding of the business and that's when the company really took off and started to change in positive ways. We drove the company from 2000 to 2019, diversifying our product range and substantially growing the business, adding major new clients including Boeing, Lockheed Martin, BAE Systems, and Rolls Royce," says Lluberes.

Prime Technology's subsequent growth was a result of the creativity and energy of its employees, a determination to bring on board new and developing technologies, and an eagerness to listen closely to what its customers wanted. "We transitioned from analog to digital and developed instrumentation and systems that exceeded expectations," says Lluberes. This change was no mean feat, as the switch from analog to digital meant a massive overhaul of Prime Technology's production lines.

Growing Prime Technology by M&A

A key factor in Prime Technology's growth was winning a contract for supplying instrumentation to the U.S. Navy's submarine and surface fleet and the Royal Navy's Astute-class submarines. A significant part of Prime Technology's growth during this period involved strategic acquisitions of other companies. "In the years that I was running the company we made four acquisitions, so we were well-versed in the process of buying a company and aware of M&A firms like Woodbridge, but had never contemplated selling," says Luis.

With retirement on the horizon and no transition plan in place, it became clear that it was time to sell. "The founder's family members weren't involved in the business, and we decided that the best option to ensure a smooth transition, serving the interests of employees and our customers, would be to sell the company," says Luis. He continues, "Having taken that decision, we recognized that the avenues we'd previously used to identify the companies we'd bought were not going to fulfil the requirements of selling our own company. That's when we found Woodbridge."

Seeing M&A from the other side of the table

Woodbridge's unique model appealed to Prime Technology's senior management. "Rather than figuring out the value of a company and trying to sell the value of the company as an asset, as we had viewed many of our acquisition targets, Woodbridge identifies a company's capabilities and what future the company has," says Luis. Lluberes recalls being impressed with the smooth and professional way that Woodbridge managed the sale of his company, global pandemic notwithstanding.

In May of 2019, Prime Technology attended Woodbridge's management meeting training, where participants are encouraged to see their business from the perspective of a potential buyer. "Having been involved in acquisitions it was fascinating for me to see the same dynamic from the other side of the table. We spent two days learning how to identify value, not just the numbers, not just as a product, but the value that our company had within it. That was an eye opener to me."

Then in 2020, the pandemic arrived and along with it came global uncertainty. However, Prime Technology stuck to their transition plan and followed through with Woodbridge's process. "We sold the company in February 2021. Considering there was a chaotic pandemic in between, I think the process went very smoothly," says Luis.

Falling back in love with your company

But sellers' remorse is a real thing and parting ways with a successful company that has been a big part of your life can be stressful. Luis shares some insights:

> *"It's a difficult decision for an owner to part ways with his company. The attachment that you develop for the company you founded goes beyond the economic benefit – it's like an organic extension of yourself. The founder was convinced he wanted to sell, but when things got real, he felt like backing away – he was scared of doing it."*

Marketing Prime Technology in preparation for its sale rekindled Lluberes' love for the company he had been with for 35 years. "When you go through the process of marketing your company, you take stock of all the wonderful things that there are about it," says Luis. Letting go is difficult, but Lluberes stresses that business owners must commit to their initial objective, or they won't get anywhere with the sale process.

A company is about more than just the owner's interests

Having successfully completed that process, Luis has sage advice for business owners who are considering selling: "If you don't have a transition plan for your business, you have to make the decision to sell. And when you've made that decision, you have to stick to that path. It's important because a company is not only about the owner's interests – it's also about the employees and their families. And it's about the customers who've been part of the journey."

It is advice that has worked very well for Prime Technology – the business has continued to expand and thrive under its new ownership. The continued success of the company might not have been possible without the recognition that a succession plan was needed and a commitment to the transition to a new generation of leadership, while preserving the unique proposition that Prime Technology had created under the Luis Lluberes' guidance.

February 2021

PRIME TECHNOLOGY

Prime Technology, LLC
North Branford, Connecticut

was acquired by

COX & COMPANY

Cox & Company, Inc.
Plainview, New York

The undersigned acted as advisor to Prime Technology, LLC

WOODBRIDGE
International

1764 Litchfield Turnpike | Suite 250 | New Haven, CT 06525
203.389.8400 | woodbridgegrp.com

Chapter 4

> "A true entrepreneur runs his company and builds his company, and he's always going to be there. I was very blessed to have my wife always behind me."

Steven Childs
Paragon Corvette Reproductions

Paragon Corvette Reproductions
AUTOMOTIVE PARTS MANUFACTURING

Steven Childs knows cars. Before entering the Corvette part reproduction and restoration business, the President of Paragon Corvette Reproductions would buy cars, refurbish them, and sell them at a profit. "I've owned many, many cars in my day," says Steven.

In 1993, Steven was recruited to Paragon Corvette Reproductions Inc., a retailer and distributor of out-of-production parts for vintage Corvettes. He had such a keen interest in the company that his goal was to purchase it from the get-go. When the existing management's desire to grow the business began to wane, Steven saw his chance. In March 2002, the automobile enthusiast bought Paragon Corvette with his wife Stacey and two close friends. Steven was thrilled that what was once a passion he pursued outside of business hours had become a business – "a hobby gone mad," as he puts it.

Shifting up a gear on the road to success

The long-time lover of cars was now a business owner and recognized the growth potential his newly acquired company represented. Continual market research provided Steven and his team with the knowledge they needed to grow and meet customer demands. "We knew that there was a lot of market available to expand the company very rapidly," says Steven.
He also realized the importance of taking care of his employees. Manufacturing vintage car parts is a niche business and keeping employee turnover to an absolute minimum is vital to preserving the expertise that ongoing training creates.

Steven's business philosophy guided Paragon Corvette's expansion: Supply the best quality vintage car parts and provide customer service that exceeds that of the competition. There is only a certain amount of business per year in the car industry, and to secure valuable repeat revenue Steven had to get himself into gear and provide excellent customer service, top-quality products and competitive prices. "Those were the avenues we felt were our strongest points – we built off of that and were able to start pulling a lot of the business our way, because of those business practices," says Steven.

However, the road ahead wasn't always smooth. Steven had to deal with lawsuits from the previous owners, and market fluctuations in the aftermath of the 9/11 attack on the World Trade Center. "There was the stress of trying to build a business despite these obstacles that truly never should have been there. But that's called life and business," says Steven.

Taking center stage with "Rex"

Soon after taking over Paragon Corvette, Steven built a car for his wife, Stacey. The restoration project was documented online and in a number of industry publications, and generated huge interest in the company undertaking it. "We were able to bring this car out of a field and put it all back together into this beautiful 1958 Corvette," says Steven. Stacey named the 1958 Corvette "Rex" (adapted from "resurrected"). Rex still stands in the company showroom as an example of Paragon Corvette's determination and skill. "It really showed the industry that we knew what we were doing," says Steven.

An M&A firm that thinks outside the box

In 2016, Steven's good friend and business partner passed away. The loss acted as a catalyst for Steven's thoughts about selling Paragon Corvette – at that point, he was working across most of the company's departments, and felt that he wouldn't be able to take Paragon Corvette to the next level by himself. "We got the company to a point where we had the best reputation in the industry. Our sales were increasing," Steven recalls. He contracted an M&A firm to sell Paragon Corvette, but after none of the bids in the first round of marketing worked out, the firm told him that their portfolio was exhausted. It was then that Steven contacted Woodbridge International.

He highlights the importance of how Woodbridge thinks out of the box in terms of their mass-marketing auction-style process: "Even if a company is not in our industry, they might still be interested in us because we are a very profitable business with a great reputation and a great brand name," says Steven. By sending Paragon Corvette's blind executive teaser to the firm's thousands of contacts, Steven's company got maximum marketing exposure.

Woodbridge's management meeting training prepared Steven to go to market with Paragon Corvette. He recalls how interacting with other business owners during the management meeting training sessions helped mentally prepare him for the endeavor that is due diligence and made him realize he wasn't alone. Like Steven, the other owners attending the training wanted to leave their employees in safe hands and ensure that their brand names and legacies were respected post-sale.

Seeing the number of letters of intent that came in for Paragon Corvette made Steven realize how valuable his company truly was. "Everybody's nervous when you're starting out – how is your business going to be received in the marketplace? Once you start getting multiple NDAs and then multiple LOIs, your nerves go more toward excitement," he says.

Keep your emotions in check

Reflecting on the process with Woodbridge International, Steven notes that the firm pushes from all four corners, and that sticking to the timeline is very important. "You have to keep in mind the point of what [Woodbridge] is doing. In the Woodbridge phrase, time kills deals," he said.

The vintage car aficionado says that when you own and run a company, you never have an end date. "I needed to put our business up for sale, so I could get myself an end date," says Steven, adding that when selling a business, entrepreneurs need to keep their emotions in check. "People interested in buying, they're going to ask questions that might make you feel uncomfortable. You have to keep an open mind and not be headstrong," he reflects.

In June 2021, Paragon Corvette Reproductions Inc. was acquired by Legendary Companies and Irving Place Capital. "They truly respect our process and our company. They haven't walked in and tried to change everything, but instead learned our way," says Steven.

WOODBRIDGE
International

Mergers & Acquisitions Since 1993

Visit us: woodbridgegrp.com

Dear Sean,

As the economy continues to rebound, one positive thing we've seen is continued interest for quality well-run businesses as strategic and financial buyers aggressively acquire companies.

As a response to many questions owners have about selling their business, we are providing you with a complimentary copy of the sixth book in our series — *"Selling Your Passion – How 8 Business Owners Transformed Their Lives."*

This book will share the stories of 8 business owners who achieved the greatest sale of their lives, how they creatively packaged their business, and ensured they were well rewarded for the hard work and years they put into building their dream, and more.

It is a very active market and you might even be speaking with a buyer now. Without having competition for your business, odds are it is highly unlikely that this buyer will be the best fit and have the best terms and price

If you would like to discuss your options and when your timing makes the most sense, please give me a call or email. We are even happy to offer you a free value assessment.

Sincerely,

Don

Don Krier

Managing Director
Woodbridge International
dkrier@woodbridgegrp.com
203.389.8400 ext. 201

1764 Litchfield Turnpike, Suite 250, New Haven, CT 06525

Selling Paragon Corvette has given its owners time to travel

While he continues to run Paragon Corvette for an agreed-upon transition period, selling the company has allowed Steven and his wife to think about traveling – something they didn't have the time to do before. "I've never had more than seven consecutive days off in my entire life. I'm looking forward to just having some time off," says Steven.

Steven has valuable advice for fellow entrepreneurs: "Truly analyze [your] reasons for selling. Don't make a hasty decision. Talk it through." He uses the analogy of a car in relation to selling a company: "Take your car and polish it, clean it up, make sure it's running nice and smooth before you put the 'For Sale' sign in it. We all know a car that runs but is dirty is never going to sell for as much as a shiny car. A shiny car sells better," says Steven.

June 2021

Paragon Corvette Reproductions | Swartz Creek, MI

was acquired by

Coker Tire | Chattanooga, TN

A subsidiary of

Legendary Companies | Chattanooga, TN

A portfolio company of

Irving Place Capital | New York, NY

The undersigned acted as advisor to Paragon Corvette Reproductions

WOODBRIDGE
International

1764 Litchfield Turnpike | Suite 250 | New Haven, CT 06525
203.389.8400 | woodbridgegrp.com

Chapter 5

> "People are most happy when they're helping others, and when an entrepreneur does that, they elevate themselves, but they elevate people around them as well."

John (Jack) Casey
Northeast Work & Safety Boats

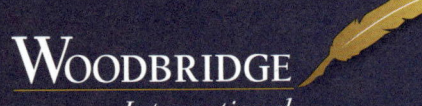

WOODBRIDGE
International
Mergers & Acquisitions Since 1993

Northeast Work & Safety Boats
RIVER & MARINE SERVICES

A near-fatal accident at the Charter Oak Bridge in Hartford, Connecticut, acted as the catalyst for John (Jack) Casey and his brother Joe to start Mainstream Water Safety Services, which later became Northeast Work & Safety Boats. Linda Casey, Jack's wife, founded Northeast Work & Safety Boats in 2001, and was joined in the business by her husband in 2004. The couple have spent their lives around water and have come to respect its beauty, as well as its potential for danger.

For over 20 years, Northeast Boats has been supplying safety and support services to construction, bridge inspection, and rehabilitation crews, operating primarily on the north-eastern seaboard of the U.S.

The perfect combination of skills

Linda, who graduated from college with a degree in mathematics and computer science, worked in the IT industry for several years before deciding to focus on raising her children. She later began working part time for a company that provided boat services to the construction industry and containment booms to oil companies.

Jack is a qualified lifeguard, rescue swimmer and a skilled boat operator. In 1975, Jack established a canoe and kayak rental business with his brother Joe. The brothers ran Mainstream Canoes together for eight years before Joe left in 1983. Jack then continued running the business for another 30 years before eventually selling it in 2013. A qualified operating engineer with Local 478 (the local chapter of the International Union of Operating Engineers Connecticut), Jack has operated tug, safety, push, and inspection boats.

The difficulties of being a pioneer

"My older brother was working for a construction company operating a safety boat, and that gave me the idea to start Mainstream Water Safety Services," says Jack of the establishment of the company that eventually grew to become became Northeast Boats. "There was no track record of businesses like ours – it wasn't a restaurant or trucking company," says Jack. Being a pioneer presented unexpected hurdles, and the Northeast Boats team faced several challenges in establishing the company. Finance providers were slow to understand the value of Jack and Linda's vision and were initially hesitant to back the venture.

Getting insurers on board also proved problematic. The entrepreneurs needed insurance providers to recognize their right to provide services that would be covered by the Good Samaritan Act, a law which gives "legal protection to people who give reasonable assistance to those who are, or whom they believe to be injured, ill, in peril, or otherwise incapacitated."

The unique nature of the company and the service it was planning to provide rendered necessary niche certifications and legal requirements such as CPR certificates, special worker's compensation, and liability insurance to rescue people underwater. "It took us about three months, and in the end, we went to the Commissioner of Medicaid Insurance to get approved," says Jack.

"Health and safety were also difficult," he continues – "we had to get certified with the American Red Cross."

Innovation that led to elevation

The inspection, rehabilitation, and repair of public infrastructure such as highway bridges is mandated by the U.S. federal government. Inspection and construction crews need access to all areas of the bridge, including the underside of the structure, below the roadway. Crews often make use of ladders, trucks with crane arms or bucket trucks to reach sections that are not easily accessible. Boats have also been used to access the underside of these bridges. However, the improvised devices attached to boats are often unstable, especially in rivers with strong currents, waves or tidal changes, creating a high-risk environment for crews.

Having spent many years operating water safety services, and aware of all the potential dangers inspection and construction crews faced, Northeast Boats was at the right place at the right time to provide a highly efficient service backed by their years of expertise. A surge in demand for the inspection and rehabilitation of public infrastructure, with 37% of bridges in the U.S. requiring maintenance, rehabilitation or repair, saw federal budgets earmarked for maintenance rather than new construction.

Further success for Northeast Boats came from the design of a patented safety boat, the Aqua Lift, which provided construction workers with safe access to inaccessible sections of bridges. The boat's special bucket lift ensured that bridge construction and inspection teams were safe and secure while completing their work.

And the need for the unique design was evidenced in the money it brought in for the company – in its first 14 months of operation, the Aqua lift generated $400,000 in revenue for Northeast Boats. This innovation really set the company apart from competitors. By the time it was sold, the company had 90% market share in five states on the north-eastern seaboard and 75% repeat business with margins of 25–50%.

Finding a firm that can support you

After running the company for over two decades, Jack and Linda decided it was time to sell. After working with a small-scale M&A firm who, as Jack recalls, "were in over their heads and weren't able to get [a deal] done for us," the couple were pointed in the direction of Woodbridge International by their wealth manager at Royal Bank of Canada. After learning that a tailor-made three-minute marketing video would form part of the Northeast Boats' marketing collateral, Jack and Linda decided to work with the M&A firm.

Selling a company isn't a walk in the park, as Jack can attest to: "It was a very arduous process…there was a lot of prep…a lot of due diligence…a lot of work. A lot of work. But [Woodbridge] had the experience, and they guided us along the way." Part of the guidance provided by Woodbridge took the form of management meeting training, wherein sellers are encouraged to see their companies from a potential buyer's perspective. "We thought the preparation that was provided was excellent. We learned what the value of our company was," says Jack.

A buyer should share your values

For Jack and Linda, it was most important that their employees, many of whom had been with the company for over a decade, be kept on and their knowledge and expertise respected. "We didn't want to lose any of our employees…they are part of your family, you're friends with them, you know, they've worked for you for 10 years or 20 years," recalls Jack. Northeast Work & Safety Boats was acquired by Capital Infrastructure Group Inc. in June 2021. Of the buyer, Jack says, "We wanted someone who was going to have a passion for [the company] and the wherewithal to move [it] forward."

While Jack admits that the entrepreneur in him worries about how to survive without the pressure and constant interaction of running a business, he has no regrets. His advice to people considering selling their businesses is simple: "Engage the services of Woodbridge. They are super professional. They stay focused on closing the sale."

June 2021

NORTHEAST
WORK & SAFETY BOATS, LLC

Northeast Work & Safety Boats, LLC

New Hartford, Connecticut

was acquired by

CAPITAL
INFRASTRUCTURE GROUP INC.

Capital Infrastructure Group, Inc.

Ontario, Canada

The undersigned acted as advisor to Northeast Work & Safety Boats, LLC

WOODBRIDGE
International

1764 Litchfield Turnpike | Suite 250 | New Haven, CT 06525
203.389.8400 | woodbridgegrp.com

Chapter 6

"I gave up a top job at a Fortune 500 company to do what I love."

Peter Jordan
Knowledge Matters

Knowledge Matters
IT SERVICES

Peter Jordan, founder and president of Knowledge Matters, loved computers from the moment he was first introduced to one in sixth grade.

In his teens, Peter taught himself to program rudimentary games. He describes the virtual world as a creative one, where he could make things "that would actually run – you weren't just writing an equation that was static."

His passion for invention was partly inspired by his father, an aircraft engineer who became an inventor after retiring. Their family home was never blown up during an experiment gone wrong, but Peter remembers that his father once tried to create a new type of snow for ski slopes and instead coated the driveway in an inch of ice.

While studying toward an MBA at Harvard, Peter became fascinated by economic modeling:

> *"There were lots of classical graphs in economics, but they were just static things…and now we had the ability to create these little working models of the world where you could test out what would happen if you had more suppliers – would the price actually go down?"*

After completing his MBA, Peter climbed the corporate ladder at Digital Equipment Corporation, a major computer manufacturer. His path to the top seemed clear – as one of the only MBAs at the company, Peter worked directly with the company's CFO and its President. As a top executive, however, he had to handle his share of tricky tasks. When Digital was going through tough times, it was Peter's job to inform the French subsidiary about the parent company's decision to downsize.

The SimCity brainwave for the learning of the future

Retrenching people in France, a country with a history of strong trade unions and labor rights, "is not something you want to be doing," says Peter. Flying home, he remembers thinking that despite being in line for the CFO position at a Fortune 500 company, his heart was not in it. He wanted to create products. Soon after getting back to the U.S., he spotted one of Digital's engineers playing SimCity and was inspired to start his own simulation-based company, namely Knowledge Matters. The brainchild that led to Knowledge Matters was born.

Knowledge Matters creates simulations that allow students to solve real-world problems through simulated scenarios covering a wide range of industries including hospitality, fashion, retail, financial markets, and manufacturing. Students learn by doing – creative thinking, experimentation, and making mistakes are encouraged.

Even in 1997, Peter knew that visual learning tools had massive potential. Business studies was (and remains) the most popular college major in the U.S. and the path was wide open for Knowledge Matters' innovative learning methods to be used in schools, corporations, and even prisons. Peter wrote the code and did the graphics for his first simulation himself, because money was tight. His wife thought he was crazy – they still joke about his quitting a six-figure job to relearn how to program.

"Teachers loved simulation learning"

To grow the company, Peter needed capital. He had been attending an entrepreneurship forum at MIT for four years when he heard about the federal government's Small Business Innovation Research grants. His application was successful, and in 1999 when Knowledge Matters' flagship product was ready for release, a childhood friend quit his high-level banking job and joined Peter's fledgling company.

The pair of former executives hit the road, introducing teachers to the business concept simulations. "Fortunately for us, they loved it," says Peter. He describes how hungry the market was for Knowledge Matters' products:

> *From there on out, it was always a matter of…how many of these could we build? How big did we want to go? I knew that I didn't love the politics of a very large company. Over the next 20 years, we tried to keep the company small but nimble while supplying products to a market that seemed able to consume pretty much everything we had the time to build."*

Selling a wildly popular company

When Knowledge Matters was sold in May 2021, the company had just 15 employees. Peter's recruitment policy was simple: hire great people and let them do great things. The formula was successful, and in 2007, the company's personal finance simulation became a national bestseller. Ten years later, in 2017, Knowledge Matters entered the U.S. college market with a collection of marketing case simulations.

Knowledge Matters had been approached by interested buyers before Peter and his business partner decided to investigate two M&A firms, one of which was Woodbridge International. In the end, they decided to go with Woodbridge for three reasons: its marketing strategy, the team's enthusiasm, and the bespoke video Woodbridge includes in its marketing collateral.

"It's more than a transaction for Woodbridge"

The first company examined by Peter relied on a traditional investment banking marketing method, and had a relatively small pool of contacts, whereas Woodbridge cast a wide net and sent blind teasers to thousands of potential buyers.

Peter adds that although the other M&A firm was "perfectly polite," it seemed like a transaction to them. Conversely, the Woodbridge team was excited about Knowledge Matters. "If they had that kind of enthusiasm for the business, it was going to show through," Peter says.

As the founder of a simulation and educational gamification company, the three-minute company video that Woodbridge produces was a critical component for him:

> "I would always [say] with our customers, once somebody sees it, they get it, and so [the video] appealed to me. I knew if we could get in front of them and they could see it moving, they would understand what we were trying to do."

Woodbridge's two-day Management Meeting Training reminded Peter of his days at Harvard, where he was asked rapid-fire questions about case studies. This time, however, the case study was his own company.

When Knowledge Matters went to market, the blind teaser attracted close to 80 bids. Peter says he felt overwhelmed but incredibly flattered, and leaned on Woodbridge's expertise to decide which bidders were worth meeting. He also appreciated that the closing team kept him to the strict 150-day deadline, joking that he is something of a procrastinator.

Woodbridge facilitated the deal between Knowledge Matters and eDynamic Learning and Gauge Capital in May 2021, at a time when nearly 100% of teachers were using tech to engage with their students.

Flying off to new adventures

Peter is currently working through his 12-month transition period – he was adamant during the pre-market phase that he could not up and leave the "millions of kids" who rely on Knowledge Matters' products.

Peter has big plans for the future. His three kids are at colleges in California, Montana, and North Carolina. He and his wife plan to spend time near their kids and explore the world outside of New England.

Since the sale, Peter has had the time to take flying lessons, following in his daughter's footsteps. She got her pilot's license at 17, and he wants to be with her in the cockpit should anything go wrong.

Describing the M&A process as stressful, Peter's advice to business owners looking to sell is to be very cautious when picking the firm they choose to work with. Peter notes that the firm should be "really enthusiastic about the business," and points out that Woodbridge kept the pressurized proceedings "positive."

May 2021

Knowledge Matters | Hadley, Massachusetts

was acquired by

eDynamic Learning | Southlake, Texas

a portfolio company of

Gauge Capital | Dallas, Texas

The undersigned acted as advisor to Knowledge Matters

WOODBRIDGE
International

1764 Litchfield Turnpike | Suite 250 | New Haven, CT 06525
203.389.8400 | woodbridgegrp.com

Chapter 7

> "I think about all the people that need this company to pay their mortgages; it's exciting to me that we are responsible for their livelihoods. It's a humbling thing, in a sense, that they've trusted me. So, it's my responsibility to make sure the company survives."

Phil Brothers
Amuze Products

WOODBRIDGE
International
Mergers & Acquisitions Since 1993

Amuze Products
VENDING SERVICES

Phil Brothers always knew that he didn't like working for other people. The serial entrepreneur recognized early on that he could do whatever his bosses were doing and do it better. "I wanted to learn how to make the decisions because I wanted to be able to affect my own life instead of someone else telling me what to do," recalls the CEO and founder of Amuze Products, a market-leading vending massage chair provider.

From nonprofit to hi-tech

After working in the nonprofit space for a period, Phil realized he needed more income security and started his first vending-machine company selling snack foods like M&Ms and nuts. A friend gave Phil startup advice that he would only later learn wasn't particularly good: "I eventually sold that business because it was just too hard. It was really difficult to make money. I wouldn't find out the correct way to do vending until later in life," says Phil of his first venture.

Next, he took a sales job in Silicon Valley, at the start of the tech boom. It was the era of Web 1.0, and there was a lot of money flying around. "Everybody's giving these guys who had no reason to have money, money…They're making all these crazy decisions, and I'm realizing, 'What am I doing here?' These guys can't make a decision to save their lives," says Phil of a time he describes as "the wild west."

The market downturn of 2001–2002 precipitated Phil's leaving tech and reentering the vending business, this time with a focus on placing vending machines in malls. By this time, entrepreneurship was an integral part of Phil's identity, and when he sold the mall vending company, he soon started up a digital advertising firm. "That was a big one. We were raising a lot of money from venture capital, and going strong, but we started in 2006. And remember what happened a couple years later?"

The nature of startups

The 2008 financial crisis was the end of Phil's most successful venture yet – like millions of Americans, he sold whatever he could to stay afloat – "I was literally selling my couches to pay rent, I was selling whatever I had just to make rent. That was a rough time," says Phil. Six months later he started up a new venture. Out of the 6,000 accounts his digital advertising company had acquired, one remained – a trampoline park. "It was a completely new industry… I went back to my roots and put a little candy vending machine in there, because I had some extras in a garage," says Phil. Amuze Products was born.

The machine did well, and as the trampoline park opened new locations throughout the Bay Area, Phil continued supplying their vending machines. Always alive to possibilities, Phil realized that while his vending machines were targeting the kids at the trampoline parks, their parents were another story:

"I'm looking at all the parents just sitting there doing nothing, and I'm like, 'They're just sitting there on their iPhones waiting for their kid to get done jumping! What am I going to do with these parents?' There's money there, but I couldn't figure it out. And finally, I was like, 'You know what, I bet I could put a massage chair in here.'"

Spotting the gap

Phil didn't waste time. He ordered a few used massage chairs from Craigslist and set them up in one of the trampoline parks he worked with. When he came back a few weeks later, he was blown away by how much money the chairs had made. Because the massage chairs were so profitable, the owner of the trampoline parks was willing to finance Phil. With that loan, Phil bought his first 30 chairs in May 2012, and put them in trampoline parks up and down the West Coast.

At that stage, the massage chairs only took dollar bills, so Phil had to collect the money manually by traveling from location to location. When this became too time-consuming, he began to ask people working at the trampoline parks to collect the bills for him. "I would just call people up and say, 'Can you pull the money out?', which is not a great business method," the entrepreneur admits.

By the time he'd bought a hundred chairs, Phil knew he had to improve operations. He decided to fit all the vending chairs with credit card readers that could also count bills. Of the decision, Phil says: "I could monitor the chairs and I would just start billing the location. And so, once we put these credit card readers on, that just dramatically changed the entire business."

Competition was slow to arrive

Phil had identified a niche that no one was servicing and had a huge start on his competition. So much so that for the first four years, Amuze had no competitors. At industry tradeshows, Phil barely had to sell his product, and it was all he could do to keep up with orders. By 2018, however, things had started to change. Phil's response was to "buckle down and really start selling." He hired an additional salesperson and a customer service representative who would call customers before they called Amuze. "Customer service has brought me incredible loyalty – I pick up a lot of business from my competitors," says the entrepreneur.

M&A connections

To support Amuze's growth, Phil hired a director of operations and focused on documenting all Amuze's processes and contracts. Amuze's new director of operations had worked for Fun Spot, a specialized equipment and trampoline park equipment designer, manufacturer, and distributor that had been sold by Woodbridge International in 2018. Phil had heard about the sale but hadn't thought much about it at the time. But as Amuze continued to grow, he began to consider diversifying his assets. In 2018, Phil reached out to Larry Reinharz, a partner at Woodbridge, and began to discuss the possibility of selling his company. After signing on with the firm, he went through Woodbridge's management meeting training, the aim of which is to prepare sellers for the mass-market auction process that the M&A firm uses to elicit bids – "It definitely helped us get the multiple we wanted," recalls Phil.

Amuze Products was acquired by Surge Private Equity LLC and CrowdOut Capital LLC in July 2021. Not being ready to retire, Phil structured the deal so that he would remain CEO and retain a 30% stake in the company. Selling Amuze has allowed Phil to explore other interests – "I'm investing in real estate or apartment buildings, and that's been good. I'm happy for the diversification."

Get your processes in order

Having gone through the sale process, Phil's advice for those considering selling their businesses is this: "You've got to set your company up correctly to be sold; you need to be able to show that there's still a lot of growth left in your business. Contracts have to be in place. You have to set the company up to be handled by someone else. Start putting those pieces in place so that the company can survive without you."

July 2021

Amūze Products | TURN ANY SPACE INTO PROFIT

Amuze Products Inc. | Dallas, Texas

was acquired by

SURGE PRIVATE EQUITY

Surge Private Equity LLC | Dallas, Texas

and

CrowdOut

CrowdOut Capital LLC | Austin, Texas

The undersigned acted as advisor to Amuze Products, Inc.

WOODBRIDGE
International

1764 Litchfield Turnpike | Suite 250 | New Haven, CT 06525
203.389.8400 | woodbridgegrp.com

Chapter 8

" I was able to control my own destiny and control my own working circumstances. "

Frank Cambareri
Alternative Exports

Alternative Exports
INTERNATIONAL DISTRIBUTOR

After working his way to the top of two corporations, in 2002, Frank Cambareri decided to redirect his energy and work on a business of his own, where he would be free to determine how much and how fast it should grow.

Frank's first business was a cellular phone dealership in the exciting, early days of the industry, "when they were the size of suitcases." After growing that company into a successful business, he grew tired of the industry's unpredictable growth trajectory and sold it.

Selling two-way radios in the Caribbean

It was Frank's ability to make connections and detect opportunities that led to the idea that became Alternative Exports. A friend whom he frequently visited in the Caribbean always requested that Frank bring as many two-way radios as he could carry with him – the radios cost a few dollars apiece in the U.S. but could be resold for $1,000 in the Caribbean. Seeing the hefty profits his friend was raking in, Frank had an "aha!" moment.

In 2004, he purchased Alternative Exports. At the time, it was a tiny business – the owner and a single employee were doing low volumes of trade. Frank began to streamline his newly-acquired company and took it to the next level of growth.

Coming full circle, albeit unexpectedly

Today, the company exports over 40,000 essential products (primarily manufactured by U.S. OEMs) to commercial customers in more than 30 countries in South and Central America and the Caribbean. The largest product category that Alternative Exports deals in is medical supplies, bringing Frank's medical background into play, albeit inadvertently.

Before enrolling at the University of Central Florida, where he graduated with a business degree, Frank had been attending medical school in the Dominican Republic for about two years, but left the country due to political instability.

Frank explains that the most challenging aspect of starting out was scaling the business: "When you're small and you're starting out, you have to deal with it all…vendors, suppliers, customers, traveling, sourcing products…" The logistics were complex with the company's catalog growing constantly and its customer base spanning education, hospitality, industry, construction, automotive dealerships, and retail. He describes wearing 10 different hats in the early days, juggling suppliers, customers, overseeing shipping and ensuring deliveries were made on time. Some of those early lessons were condensed into Alternative Exports' current business model. The company remains lean with a team of 24 valuable employees who, with Frank, made it a productive and profitable enterprise.

Alternative Exports benefited from the strong global demand for products made in the U.S., which are seen as high-quality and durable. In addition, the company is a renowned supplier of medical consumables – necessities that must be constantly replenished – to underserved markets. Key to the company's success is its network of over 4,500 manufacturers and vendors providing fast, efficient sourcing built by Frank and his team during the last two decades.

Recognizing when to step aside

Selling the business had always been part of his plan – and after making a good income for 18 years, Frank wanted to pursue other interests. He also wanted a strategic buyer to take Alternative Exports to its next level of growth.

"Don't go for cheap when it comes to M&A"

Woodbridge International was the second M&A firm that Frank approached. The first "didn't speak the same business language that [he] did," and had a particularly laborious process for gathering the documentation required for underwriting the deal. "It's still difficult, but the M&A firm can make it easier using the right technologies, with the right people in place to support you," Frank says.

He admits that he chose the first M&A firm for its price, balking at Woodbridge's commission, "but I realized I'll have much more support and probability of success going with Woodbridge, than going for cheap. After all, this is […] the biggest sale of my life."

The blind executive teaser that Woodbridge sent out to thousands of potential buyers initially gave Frank cause for concern. "This is my baby; there are a lot of customers and manufacturers who know me really well, but Woodbridge uses a system where I first have to approve any potential strategic buyers receiving the Confidential Information Memorandum and we managed to weed out a few people that we thought were just fishing for information," says Frank.

From one venture to the next

After Woodbridge facilitated the sale of Alternative Exports to 3T Medical Systems and Plymouth Growth Partners in July 2021, Frank says he saw the value of a buyer with a complementary product offering geared toward the same markets – they were able to step in almost immediately and leverage the capacity of the business," while Alternative Exports contributed with its distribution capabilities, licenses, authorizations, and capacity to convey products to hard-to-reach locations.

Frank says that if Alternative Exports had not sold, the company would have expanded far more slowly without the capacity that the new buyers brought in. On a personal level, "The timing was perfect for me to put into effect what my plan has always been," says Frank, describing the sale as a "milestone" and "life-changing event" that came to fruition after years of planning.

The transition period has been split into two phases: for the first 100 days, Frank worked full-time, before switching to part-time for the remainder of 2021. He is fully invested in the transition and is giving his all to the new owners, of whom he says, "They're such good people and they are a pleasure to work with." Frank plans to take a well-deserved holiday (perhaps in Greece) once the transition period is complete, before beginning his next venture.

Frank advises business owners who are thinking of selling to be realistic and ensure the company is well-structured and profitable before making the sale of a lifetime. "If your business is not organized, it will come out in the sale process. If your business is not as profitable as you're portraying it to be, it will come out in the sale process. If you are embellishing your story to make it sound better than what it is, it will come out in the sale process. So, my advice to people would be that if you have to, take a year or take a couple of years and work on things."

July 2021

ALTERNATIVE EXPORTS
GLOBAL SOLUTIONS FOR BUSINESS & INDUSTRY

Alternative Exports, Inc. | Apopka, Florida

has been acquired by

3T MEDICAL SYSTEMS

3T Medical Systems | Canton, Michigan

a portfolio company of

PLYMOUTH GROWTH

Plymouth Growth Partners | Ann Arbor, Michigan

The undersigned acted as advisor to Alternative Exports, Inc.